INSIDE THE INDUSTRY
GREEN JOBS

BY COURTNEY FARRELL

INSIDE THE INDUSTRY
GREEN JOBS

BY COURTNEY FARRELL

Content Consultant
Caroline J. Russ, EMBA
On-Campus Job Placement Specialist
Career Development Center, Florida State College at Jacksonville

ABDO
Publishing Company

CREDITS

Published by ABDO Publishing Company, 8000 West 78th Street, Edina, Minnesota 55439. Copyright © 2011 by Abdo Consulting Group, Inc. International copyrights reserved in all countries. No part of this book may be reproduced in any form without written permission from the publisher. The Essential Library™ is a trademark and logo of ABDO Publishing Company.

Printed in the United States of America,
North Mankato, Minnesota
112010
012011

 THIS BOOK CONTAINS AT LEAST 10% RECYCLED MATERIALS.

Editor: Mari Kesselring
Copy Editor: David Johnstone
Interior Design and Production: Emily Love
Cover Design: Emily Love

Library of Congress Cataloging-in-Publication Data
Farrell, Courtney.
  Green jobs / by Courtney Farrell.
      p. cm. -- (Inside the industry)
  Includes bibliographical references.
  ISBN 978-1-61714-801-9
 1. Occupations--Juvenile literature. 2. Vocational guidance--Juvenile literature. 3. Environmental protection--Juvenile literature. I. Title.
  HF5381.2.F37 2011
  331.702--dc22
                              2010039122

TABLE OF CONTENTS

President Barack Obama toured the solar panels at Nellis Air Force Base in Nevada on May 27, 2009, in an effort to promote renewable energy.

IS A GREEN JOB FOR YOU?

"We cannot drill our way to energy independence, but must fast-track investments in renewable sources of energy like solar power, wind power and advanced biofuels. . . . It's a strategy that will create millions of new jobs that pay well and

cannot be outsourced, and one that will leave our children a world that is cleaner and safer."[1]
—*Barack Obama, July 17, 2008*

Are you passionate about protecting the planet? Do you want your job to make a difference? Young people all over the world realize the planet is in crisis, and they are rising to the challenge. When they graduate, they won't just be looking for jobs—they will be looking for green jobs. If you are one of these young people, a green job is waiting for you. But how do you get there? This book is your road map to success in the green industry.

Green jobs benefit the environment. If you get one, you will do more for the planet than signing an occasional petition. In the areas of renewable energy, green building, recycling, or any other aspect of sustainable living, you will make a real impact on the world. The key is to figure out which area is right for you. In this book, we will take a whirlwind tour of green job prospects and then look closely at four of them: green architect, organic farmer, professional conservationist, and alternative energy expert. You will find out what each job entails and how to prepare for it.

A GREEN DREAM JOB

Just for fun, let's start with a high-profile green job: National Geographic explorer-in-residence. Dereck and Beverly Joubert make a living from their passion for conservation. Through films, photography, and writing, the Jouberts bring the wilderness of Africa to living rooms around the world.

A male lion takes down a water buffalo in Botswana, where a National Geographic program is working to save declining lion populations.

The Jouberts live and work in Botswana, where wild lion populations are in decline. Expanding human populations have brought the Masai people and lions into conflict. Domestic cattle are easier prey than Cape buffalo, so lions will eat them if they get a chance. The Masai traditionally kill lions if they lose a cow to one, but Beverly and Dereck are working to change that. Through a National Geographic program called The Big Cat Initiative, herders who lose a cow to large predators are generously compensated through donations and grants. The Masai are paid quarterly, but only if no one kills a lion during that part of the year. Beverly Joubert describes how successful the program has been:

Five years prior to us going in, there were 450 lions in this area. They killed 250 of them in the five years. We've been supporting this project for two years now, and only four lions have been killed. So that's a remarkable difference.[2]

The Jouberts probably have the greenest jobs ever, but being green doesn't have to mean that you live on a shoestring budget. They market their books and films and Beverly's stunning photographs. They're living proof that you can do good in the world while doing well for yourself.

A SURVEY OF GREEN JOBS

Realistically, your chances of becoming a conservationist with a television show are slim. So, what other options are there? Green jobs exist to meet each of society's needs. For instance, people need food, and that food can be produced organically instead of chemically. Shelter can come in the form of sustainably built green buildings instead of conventional ones. Solar and wind energy can replace fossil fuels. If every problem is an opportunity, then there are a lot of opportunities for green jobs in the world.

You can probably list several green jobs off the top of your head. But there are many jobs that you might not realize are green. Jobs such as recycler, company sustainability coordinator, and solar panel installer are green. Other green careers may be even less obvious. For instance, attorneys can be green if environmental law is their focus. "Sometimes you need to go to court to make sure that going green happens," says Bill Funk, an environmental law professor at Lewis and

More students like Jackie Blizzard, a civil engineering student at Clemson University, are hoping to find green jobs once they enter the workforce.

Clark Law School in Portland, Oregon.[3]

Law is one of the invisible structures that holds our society together, as are banking, corporate policy making, and international treaties. The term *invisible structures* applies to all the cultural and financial practices

AN INTERNSHIP IN ENVIRONMENTAL LAW

Internships can be a great way for students to see whether a particular career choice is the right one. Think you might be interested in environmental law? Apply for a summer internship at a nonprofit organization such as the Environmental Defense Fund or Earthjustice. It just might lead you to a permanent job.

that affect the environment. In a classic example, banks often deny construction loans for innovative green homes but finance industries such as mining and logging, which can be ecologically destructive. People in politics, law, and finance can change unsustainable policies like these, making their jobs the greenest of all.

When you're choosing an environmentally responsible career, remember two things. First, inventive people can make any career a green job. If the career that really excites you is in a traditionally nongreen field, why not be the first person to change it? Second, keep in mind that not all companies that sound green really are. It all depends on the way they are managed. Being green is good for business, so unscrupulous companies may try to look green when they're not. It's difficult to investigate a company when you've just received a job offer, so check them out early—before you interview. Do everything you can to work toward the green job of your dreams.

TEN POPULAR GREEN JOBS

Are you ready to explore which green jobs are good fits for you? This book will cover the following jobs in depth: green architect, organic farmer, professional conservationist, and alternative energy expert. But first, here is a list of other popular jobs in the field.

1. Ecotourism: The movement started with small groups touring natural areas, but now the entire hospitality industry is greening fast. People working in ecotourism work at hotels or resorts that are green.

2. Sustainability coordinator: Large corporations looking to go green now hire full-time professionals to organize everything from office recycling to product packaging.

3. City planning professional: These professionals design urban areas that encourage walking, biking, and local shopping.

4. Sustainability educator: Teachers and professors are needed at all levels, from summer nature programs for kids up to college ecology courses.

5. Hydrologist: A hydrologist studies the movement and distribution of water supplies as well as the quality of

You can help save the planet by recycling old cell phones to keep them out of landfills.

that water. Hydrologists are increasingly in demand to help us make the best use of our water supply.

6. Waste disposal specialist: Industrial chemicals were once dumped in waterways, causing cancer clusters in local communities. Now chemical disposal is tightly regulated. Experts design safe disposal methods for chemical, biological, and radioactive waste.

7. Electric vehicle electrician: One major green initiative in the past few years has been the creation of vehicles that run on electricity instead of gasoline. This reduces the need to drill for oil, which can destroy

natural areas. Electricians are needed to repair these vehicles when they break down.

GREEN OR GREEN-WASHED?

Sometimes, companies that look green on the surface aren't really green at all. One of these green-washed companies is Diamond Wire Material Technologies, a Colorado-based solar panel maker. In 2010, investigators discovered that a Diamond Wire employee had dumped toxic waste in a pond for more than one year, threatening local wells. The manufacturing of all solar panels is a toxic process, but truly green solar companies dispose of their waste properly.

8. Animal conservationist: An animal conservationist can help animals from becoming extinct by lobbying for laws that protect the animals and staging protests and spreading knowledge to inform the public of the dangers some species face.

9. Camp counselor: Camp counselors can teach young children to appreciate and respect nature. They can inspire the next generation of green workers.

10. Park ranger: National, state, county, and municipal parks throughout the United States preserve areas of nature that people can visit. Park rangers make sure visitors follow the rules to keep parks safe and orderly for generations of visitors.

Park rangers work in parks all over the country.

The green industry holds abundant opportunities for career paths. Read on to find out how you can become a part of this exciting movement. Green architects are working to change the face of residential and commercial building. Organic farmers are growing healthy crops without the use of pesticides. Professional conservationists are preserving and protecting nature. And, finally, alternative energy experts are promoting renewable sources of energy. There has never been a better time to join the green industry.

This energy efficient office building in Vermont uses solar panels, a cooling pond, and other green features.

WHAT IS A GREEN ARCHITECT?

Architects design buildings, drawing plans that serve as instruction manuals for construction crews. An architect can be green or not, depending on the designs and building materials used. A green architect chooses sustainable, nontoxic materials to build energy-efficient buildings. People are especially interested in green building these days because of some problems discovered in conventional buildings.

One problem with conventional buildings is the high level of toxins in common construction materials. Materials such as vinyl and plywood can outgas, which means they emit small quantities of poisonous chemicals into the air. The chemicals accumulate in the air inside buildings, which can cause cancer and other health problems. For example, the PVC (polyvinyl chloride) used to make carpet, flooring, and pipes leaches out toxins called phthalates. Manufacturers use phthalates to make plastics pliable, but phthalates cause liver cancer and male reproductive abnormalities. Some types of drywall used in housing construction have also been found to emit toxins. A green architect avoids toxins by using natural building materials such as adobe, bamboo, and wood.

Another problem with older, conventional buildings is their poor energy efficiency. In the past, energy was cheap, so efficiency wasn't an issue. It was easier to put in a big furnace to heat a house than it was to install extra insulation. Now energy is expensive, and we're concerned about the pollution and global warming caused by burning fossil fuels. Well-insulated homes are in demand. Green architects make sure their buildings are well insulated to reduce heating and cooling costs. Architecture is influenced by the building's location, too. In cold climates, green architects design rooms that have large south-facing windows. This is called "passive-solar design," and it takes advantage of free winter heat from the sun. Measured overhangs above windows keep the summer sun out. In warm climates, designers include shady trees outside and place windows to catch prevailing breezes.

Green builders consider sustainability when choosing materials as well. A material is considered sustainable if its embodied energy—the energy needed to acquire, manufacture, transport, and assemble it—is low. Conventional building materials have high-embodied energies, so green builders avoid them. For the same reason, green builders prefer local materials over imported ones, as local materials require less energy for shipping.

Renewable resources such as straw, adobe, and Forest Stewardship Council (FSC) certified wood are other green choices. They're considered renewable because we can use them indefinitely as long as we replant the trees and straw.

WHAT IS FSC CERTIFIED WOOD?

You might have seen lumber for sale stamped with the FSC logo. This means that the Forest Stewardship Council certified that the wood came from sustainably managed forests. Using FSC certified wood is the green way to go!

WHAT IS A GREEN ARCHITECT'S WORK ENVIRONMENT?

Architects work on computers in offices, using computer-aided design and drafting (AutoCAD) and building information modeling (BIM) programs. They take breaks from design work to meet with colleagues and clients and to visit construction sites. Some architects open their own businesses. Others find jobs with existing firms. Most professionals work a standard 40-hour workweek unless they're racing to meet a deadline. When deadlines loom they have to put in some overtime, working evenings and even occasional weekends.

HOW IS THE JOB MARKET FOR GREEN ARCHITECTS?

In 2010, there were approximately 101,000 architects working in the United States. Only some of those were practicing green architects. That year, their salaries typically ranged from approximately $42,320 to $122,640 annually.[1] Of course, a few big names earn much more, but they are the exceptions, not the rule. Women and Hispanics are underrepresented in the field. Only approximately 25 percent of architects are female.[2] Only 8 percent are Hispanic.[3] This is good news if you are female or Hispanic, and interested in architecture. Scholarships are often offered to members of underrepresented groups seeking to join certain professions.

For graduating architects, the prospects look good. The US Department of Labor estimated that demand for architects would increase by 16 percent between 2008 and 2018.[4] Demand for green architects is expected to increase even more as environmental awareness grows. This projection will be influenced by economic factors, since new construction declines during recessions. Recessions will disproportionately affect younger architects and those with less training because low-level design jobs may be outsourced to other nations.

Just remember, architecture is a field that you should pursue for love, not for money. "Architects with a master's [degree] might enter the work force with between $50,000 and $80,000 in student loan debt," explained Jeanne Sahadi, CNN/Money senior writer.[5] In fact, architecture made Sahadi's list of the three jobs that pay the least relative to the educational investment needed to land them. That doesn't necessarily matter to professionals who genuinely love their field. They make a comfortable living while spending their time doing something they are passionate about.

A PROFILE OF A GREEN ARCHITECT

There was no such thing as green architecture when Derek Trost attended the University of Oregon, but an interest in sustainability was already there. Trost learned about energy

LANDSCAPE ARCHITECTURE

Landscape architects design the spaces outside buildings instead of the buildings themselves. The profession requires an artistic eye and a good working knowledge of horticulture. Landscape architects must also be observers of human behavior, because the placement of elements such as ponds and walkways affects people's movements and emotions. Landscape architects can be green or not, depending on their designs. For example, displays of nonnative plants may look beautiful but are of little use to local birds and butterflies. A green landscape architect designs enjoyable spaces that provide wildlife habitat, too.

efficiency and passive solar design alongside his traditional courses in structure and design. "We weren't really conscious of the fact that we were being pointed toward green architecture," Trost recalled.[6]

It was like starting over when Trost moved to Minneapolis, Minnesota, where green building was new. "It was really hard once we were trying to put actual buildings together," Trost said. "Finding materials was a big-time problem. These were exotic ideas."[7]

Building is a collaborative endeavor among clients, designers, and contractors. Clients looking to build green, and green architects, can still run into trouble if their contractors aren't on board. "Contractors have to make estimates and stick by them. The last thing they want is something unusual," Trost explained.[8]

What turned the situation around was the LEED program (Leadership in Environmental Energy and Design), a government-sponsored, green-building recognition certificate. The LEED program brings designers, contractors, and clients to the table up front, so fewer mistakes are made. Although not everyone agrees that LEED is helpful, some people estimate that building greener saves money in the long run.

The way Derek Trost sees it, green building has bigger challenges than finding the right materials. "We have to transform the culture," he said. "Smaller is greener, and the greenest construction is not to do anything at all."[9]

What's a green architect's idea of the ultimate green house? "Something literally alive," Trost says.[10] The concept

LEARN SPANISH

Quite a few construction workers are native Spanish speakers. A good architect doesn't just talk to the foreman—you will want to be friendly with everybody at the job site. Most high schools have a language requirement for graduation, so choose Spanish. You will be glad you did.

of living homes first appeared in science fiction, like the ideas for cell phones and space travel did. Those dreams became realities, so perhaps this one could, too. Will future architects engineer giant trees to grow with living chambers inside?

Now that would be some real green building!

A DAY IN THE LIFE OF A GREEN ARCHITECT

So, what does a green architect do on a day-to-day basis? Most architects work with teams and spend about as much time meeting with clients and colleagues as they do in design work. Imagine that a couple hires an architect to make their dream home a reality. An architect might begin the day with some introductory research about the project. Is the site suitable? Does the plan comply with building codes and zoning laws? Later, a lengthy interview is scheduled with the clients to determine their budget and lifestyle needs. The goal is to gather enough information to enable the architect to draw some preliminary designs. Generally, the architect creates several plans for the clients to choose from. The designs will all be green, but each of them will look different.

Green architects may make models of buildings they intend to create.

The architect meets with the construction bosses before they break ground. They talk over the plan so everyone is clear on what needs to be done. During the construction process, the architect continues to make frequent trips to the job site to make sure the workers are following the blueprint exactly. Here's where an architect's social skills come in: a friendly rapport with the construction crew will make everyone's job easier and more fun, too. An architect has to be able to communicate with all kinds of people—colleagues and clients alike.

TOP FIVE QUESTIONS ABOUT BECOMING A GREEN ARCHITECT

1. *How many years of college education will I need to become an architect?*

   The minimum is five years for a bachelor of architecture. A master of architecture degree can take from one to five years, depending on your prior training.

2. *I already have construction experience, and I'd like to design homes professionally. Can I just advertise and get started?*

   No, that wouldn't be legal. Buildings have to meet safety standards, so specialized training is needed to design them. If you don't want a degree in architecture, you might consider becoming a certified professional building designer (CPBD). You will still have to complete training courses, practice building design for at least six years, and pass a certification exam.

3. *I struggle with math, but I'd love to be an architect. Are there any architecture programs out there that don't require math?*

   Most architecture programs require multiple courses in algebra, geometry, and calculus. Don't give up your dream. You can take remedial classes, with tutoring if necessary, to catch up. Or you could choose a related field, such as interior design, that requires less math.

4. *What is the college curriculum like for an architecture degree?*
The curriculum varies depending on the program. Most architecture programs include the types of courses you would expect, such as building and materials construction, computer applications, design, and physics. It might also include a few that might surprise you, such as public speaking, art, and writing.

5. *Can I open my own firm immediately after I graduate with a bachelor's degree in architecture?*
Most likely you will need to find a position as an intern first. After internships, existing firms typically employ graduates. It takes an established reputation and significant financial reserves to open your own firm.

Carpentry students from Charlottesville Albemarle Technical Education Center work together building a LEED certified house.

WOULD YOU MAKE A GOOD GREEN ARCHITECT?

So you want to be an architect, but do you have the right stuff? Let's find out. If you don't have all the interests and skills that make a good architect, don't worry. Many of them can be easily developed through hard work and practice. If you don't have any of them, you might want to reconsider. Another green career could be a better fit.

Let's start by thinking about the classes you enjoy in school. Which subjects do you look forward to? Which classes do you endure, staring endlessly at the clock? Typical architects remember liking math, art, physics, and industrial technology, or "shop," classes. Architects need verbal skills, too, but these can be honed later in life. What's difficult to develop in adulthood is that knack for spatial relationships. Do you see how things fit together when others are confused? Can you clearly imagine objects in three dimensions and even rotate them mentally? If so, you're already hardwired to be good at pursuits like architecture and engineering.

Keep in mind that doing well in a class isn't exactly the same thing as liking it. If you dug deep, tried hard, and ended up with a good grade, that's great. But would you want to revisit those concepts daily? If so, carry on. You just might be a budding architect.

ARCHITECTS ARE ARTISTS, TOO!

Well-designed buildings interact constantly with their occupants and their environments. They are not only functional. They are also beautiful. To create buildings like these, architects need a strong aesthetic sense—a feeling for the shapes and angles that people find pleasing.

"Architecture is art," explains architect Richard Meier. "Every work is a work of art. Architecture is the greatest of the arts, and it encompasses thinking that other arts don't even deal with. Like relationship of the work to the individual human being—the person who uses it; the person who sees it; and how that person perceives that space."[1]

Even in this age of computer-aided design, architects still need to be able to sketch out their ideas on paper. It might surprise you that old-fashioned drawing is still in demand, but in a 2003 survey, 61 percent of employers said that sketching was the skill most lacking in new architects.[2] In meetings with clients, nothing beats a quick drawing to make sure you're both on the same page. "It is clear that architecture students need to be taught how to better share their ideas with clients, users, and the general public," said Katherine A. Bojsza, vice president of the American Institute of Architecture Students.[3]

BUILD YOUR ARTISTIC SENSE

One way to build your artistic sense is by sketching the things around you. Visit your town or city center, and find a place to sit undisturbed. Notice how each building fits into the cityscape. Do any buildings seem out of place? Sketch the ones that please you, or add your own fantasy buildings to the skyline. Sketching is a skill you will use regularly as an architect.

You will get a jump on the competition by developing the skills employers need, and few graduates have. Even if you don't consider yourself a good artist now, you have time to improve. Some degree of artistic ability is natural talent, but people really do get better with practice.

Green architects might use many windows in their designs to take advantage of natural light.

PERSUASIVE SPEAKING SKILLS

Oral and written communication are two skills that are frequently weak in young architects. Many designers are visual-spatial learners. They think more in pictures than in words. Articulating concepts verbally can be difficult for them. But to be a successful architect, you will need both skill sets. No matter how impressive your designs are, you will need people to help you build them. Inspiring others is your crucial first step. Therefore, you must learn how to effectively communicate with people.

"Architecture is a synthesis of design, problem solving, business, interpersonal communication, and collaboration, among other things. Individuals who are successful in this practice generally have the facility to nimbly move between these modes of thought," said Phil Harrison, CEO of Perkins & Will, a noted Chicago design firm.[4]

Don't panic if you're a little weak in verbal skills, especially if you have strong spatial abilities. Few people do both verbal and spatial tasks equally well. With practice, you can become an articulate writer and a persuasive speaker, too. You're already ahead of the competition now that you know what skills you need.

TRAITS OF A VISUAL-SPATIAL LEARNER

You might be a visual-spatial learner if you:

- Think more in pictures than in words
- Grasp concepts suddenly (the "lightbulb" goes on)
- See the big picture better than the details
- Enjoy math and technology
- Don't need repetition to remember material

CHECKLIST

Is a career in green architecture a good fit for you? Discover whether you've got what it takes with this checklist.

- *Do you like building things?*

- *Are you good at figuring out how things are put together?*

- *Do you have excellent math skills and enjoy math classes?*

- *Do you enjoy looking at interesting buildings and homes?*

- *Do you like drawing, painting, sculpture, or some other art hobby?*

- *Do you care about the environment and want to make healthier buildings for people to live and work in?*

If you answered yes to most of these questions, you are on the track to a career in green architecture. But even if you don't have a lot of these skills yet, you might still be a good fit. Hard work and determination can go a long way toward helping you achieve your dream job.

HOW TO GET THERE

CLASSES TO TAKE IN HIGH SCHOOL

Colleges don't just look at grades—they also consider your class choices. Did you take the easy options throughout high school, or is your transcript loaded with AP and honors classes? Enroll in those courses where you can, and don't skip the AP exam at the end. If you do well enough, those credits will transfer to colleges.

Let's take a look at the specifics. First of all, architectural colleges want to see a lot of math on your transcript. Your best bet is to take plane geometry, intermediate algebra, and trigonometry, although not every school requires all three. Top schools such as Cornell University also recommend calculus, but it's best to interpret that recommendation as a requirement. Imagine how you will rate if the other applicants took calculus and you didn't. Programs are competitive, with many more applicants than there are spaces for incoming freshmen. It's a good idea to take as many of these math classes as you can, even if the program you want to apply to doesn't specifically require them for admission.

Physics is an entrance requirement at many colleges, but you don't need classes in architecture, engineering, or drafting. Most high schools don't offer them anyway. Of course, if you get a chance to take one of these classes, it will make you a stronger applicant. Community colleges usually allow high school students to take classes before graduation, so you might pick up a

TOASTMASTERS

If you're 18 or older, the Toastmasters club can help you hone your speaking skills. During club meetings, members make speeches on topics of their choice and then receive suggestions to help them improve. The emphasis is on the positive, so you will receive supportive pointers rather than unhelpful criticism.

drafting class there. Showing early and consistent interest in the subject is one key to admission!

Finally, take a full four years of English along with at least one foreign language. The majority of colleges now require two years of foreign language for admission. Taking speech or communication classes can also help you build interpersonal communication skills.

YOUR PORTFOLIO

You will need to submit a portfolio as part of your application package, so begin planning it now. Take high-quality photographs of your sculptures, paintings, art photography, or other projects as you finish them. Make notes on each: the date, medium used, whether it was done for a class or on your own, and the original size of the piece. Write a few sentences about the inspiration or theme of the piece. Most schools require examples of freehand drawing ability, so be sure to include some. Your portfolio eventually will be a professional-looking book of photographs of your art, showing off your talent.

MAKE THE RIGHT CAREER CHOICE

Surprisingly, some college students who don't enjoy their studies never change their majors. They imagine that a job in that field will somehow be different, and they think of their classes as hurdles standing in their way. Careers actually feel a lot like the hands-on or lab courses in each major. If you like those classes, it's a good sign that you will be happy at your job later.

STANDARDIZED TESTS

In your junior or senior year, take the SAT Reasoning Test as well as the SAT Subject Test in Mathematics. For some colleges, you can substitute the ACT, but make sure to include the writing component. One advantage of the ACT is that students are allowed to take it beginning when they are in sixth grade. You can take the test several times a year, getting better and better at it with each try. The questions change from year to year, but question types stay the same.

NETWORKING NOTES

Committed networkers take notes about the people they've met and compile them into networking notebooks or electronic records. Notes include the name of the company of each professional as well as his or her contact information, but some networkers also include details such as hobbies and spouses' names. Those make great conversation starters later. Networkers e-mail or call each person in the book occasionally to stay in touch.

Additionally, many people use Web sites such as LinkedIn to network. These sites are becoming so popular that you are out of the loop if you aren't on one of them. Using them to network could lead to many exciting opportunities, but be wary of users you don't know in real life.

YOU'RE IN! NOW WHAT?

You have several pathways to choose from. One route is to take five years to get a bachelor's degree in architecture and then pass the Architectural Registration Exam (ARE). That qualifies you to work in the field but not to teach.

If you know you want a master's degree, you can take a four-year undergraduate program followed by a two- or three-year master's degree. Some universities will allow you to take some of your master's level architect courses while you are still pursuing your bachelor's degree. A master's degree qualifies you both to work in the field and to teach at a university.

A third pathway is open to those who study architecture after completing a four-year degree in another subject. Because of the lack of previous training, these students may take as long as five years to get their master's degree.

NETWORKING

Now it's time to find your first internship and, later, a real job. But how? Online job sites are worth a look, but don't rely only on them. Networking is essential—it's still who you know that matters. "As a rule of thumb, nearly 7 out of 10 jobs are landed through networking," says University of Massachusetts Lowell career counselor Priscilla March.[5]

For recent graduates, networking poses special challenges. Networking is usually a give-and-take. Professionals exchange information as well as useful contacts. But what does a young person have to offer in such a scenario? Why would a busy professional take time out of his or her day to talk on the phone or have lunch with a recent college graduate? The answer, in short, is your appreciation. Professionals remember being students themselves, and many are willing to take a few minutes to share some of their hard-earned wisdom. Remember this, and be sure to express your gratitude both verbally and in a prompt handwritten note.

Networking can be nerve-wracking at first. What if you can't think of anything to say? One good way to practice is with your teachers. An internship is the most valuable sort of networking a student can do, so you might try asking your professors whether they know of any opportunities. Ask them to listen as you try out your "elevator speech"—a 30-second bit introducing yourself and your career goal. What other professionals do they recommend? Take notes so you will have that contact information when you need it.

To begin networking, talk to everybody you know about your professional goals. You never know who may be able to provide a useful contact. Once you've identified a person you'd like to network with, the phrase to use when asking for a meeting is "informational meeting." Asking for an informational meeting indicates that you're not necessarily looking for a job, but you'd like to meet them and learn about the industry. If a professional thinks an unqualified applicant wants to meet to ask for a job, he or she will probably avoid that meeting.

Avoid cold-calls or mass e-mails. They probably won't work, and they may annoy the people you're trying to connect with. It's best to stick to people referred to you by someone you know, so you have a name to drop in the initial conversation. Even if someone does not agree to help you, thank the professional, and keep in touch. That person might be in a position to open a door for you some day.

Because part of an architect's job involves meeting with clients, people skills are important.

A tractor sprays a field of spinach with pesticides at a nonorganic farm.

WHAT IS AN ORGANIC FARMER?

WHAT IS AN
ORGANIC FARMER?

hat is the difference between an organic farmer and a conventional farmer? Conventionally grown produce is sprayed with pesticides to kill insects, herbicides to kill weeds, and fungicides to stop mold. The plants themselves may be genetically modified to survive doses of herbicides that would kill ordinary crops. On the other hand, organic farming is done without pesticides, herbicides, chemical fertilizers, or genetic modification of the plants.

Many health-conscious consumers are concerned about traces of poisons that may remain on conventional produce. Many conventional fungicides are known carcinogens, but it is still legal to use them on food crops. Since fungal diseases can destroy whole harvests, and millions of people rely on that food, fungicides remain available.

Pesticides are another problem. In addition to toxicity, some are designed to reduce insect populations by disrupting hormones that regulate breeding. Recent evidence indicates that such pesticides don't disrupt the hormones of bugs alone—they affect people and animals, too. Higher rates of cancer, birth defects, and reproductive abnormalities are just a few of the possible results. Farm workers who apply the pesticides receive the heaviest doses, but as the toxins disperse, they endanger us all.

In a 2000 to 2004 study, kids with high levels of pesticide residues in their bodies were twice as likely to have ADHD as those with no detectable exposure. "I would say buy organic as much as possible," said the study's lead author Maryse F. Bouchard. "I would also recommend washing fruits and vegetables as much as possible."[1]

Organic farms use compost instead of chemicals to return nutrients to the soil. Compost is a mixture of vegetation and manure, decomposed until it looks and smells like soil. A few inches of compost worked into the soil annually keeps soil rich by slowly releasing nutrients to plant roots. Instead of using herbicides, organic farmers block weeds by mulching bare ground with straw or wood chips. The combination of compost and mulch makes organic soil absorb moisture like a sponge. Less water runs off during storms, and valuable soil and nutrients stay put.

Conventionally farmed soil doesn't hold together the way organically farmed soil does. This makes it susceptible to erosion from rain and wind. Farmlands are degraded over time from topsoil loss, and sediments damage lakes and streams. Even light rains that don't wash away soil will mobilize chemical fertilizers, washing them into waterways.

Fertilizers, even natural ones, also create problems if they run off into water. Fertilizers cause artificially high nutrient levels in the water. In turn, this causes algae blooms, or overgrowths of algae. In a few days, when the artificially high nutrient levels decline, the algae die off. Aerobic, or oxygen-using, microorganisms that feed on the dead algae then proliferate. These microscopic creatures use up the dissolved oxygen in the water, causing fish to suffocate. This is why algae blooms are so often followed by fish kills—ecological disasters in which shorelines are covered with dead fish.

Organic farming has plenty of green advantages. By avoiding toxins, organic practices protect public health. By using compost, they protect precious topsoil as well as surrounding waterways.

You don't have to grow crops directly to be involved in organic farming. There are many related jobs that might be

More people are purchasing organic fruits and vegetables because of concerns about pesticides and herbicides.

just as satisfying. The US Department of Agriculture (USDA) operates a nationwide cooperative extension system that hires experts to help farm families with practical skills. State and federal governments hire range managers and experts in soil conservation and water quality. Individuals can create their own jobs by offering services to farmers such as hay hauling or manure removal. Sales are a growing part of organic farming, too, as the variety of natural plant care products continues to increase.

WHAT IS AN ORGANIC FARMER'S WORK ENVIRONMENT?

Organic farmers work outside most of the time. They grow crops and raise livestock such as chickens, goats, and cattle. Organic farms are surrounded by natural beauty, but there is plenty of physical labor involved. Many operations weed and harvest by hand. Most farmers don't mind that aspect of the job, which helps them stay fit. Summers are hectic, but, unless you live in a place where the growing season is year round, winters bring long periods of rest and relaxation. The pace of life in rural areas is slower than urban, and people generally take more time to chat with their neighbors. And farmers are some of the happiest people around. A 2009 survey of more than 100,000 workers found that, despite their low wages, farmers were only slightly less satisfied than top-level company executives.[2]

Farmers are businesspeople. They spend time marketing their products, attending meetings, and supervising employees. One unexpected aspect of organic farming is the possible presence of volunteers. Some city people yearn for the joys of farm life, and will volunteer to work for free just to experience it. Organizing and supervising untrained volunteers is a tricky part of the job. Volunteers need close supervision, and hosts must take special pains to make sure their guests feel appreciated. Farmers also often help neighboring farmers in exchange for help on their own farm. This is a win-win situation because both farmers benefit from skilled assistance. In fact, this "trade off" of farmwork is much more common than volunteerism.

HOW IS THE JOB MARKET FOR ORGANIC FARMERS?

Let's face it. People don't become farmers for the money. In 2008, average pay for farm managers, who run farms they don't own, was $775 per week, with those on the low end earning less than $358 weekly.[3] Earnings are reported as weekly instead of annually because so much farm work is seasonal. For comparison, these figures translate to $17,576 to $40,300 per year, but seasonal farm workers really make much less

> ## WILLING WORKERS ON ORGANIC FARMS
>
> Willing Workers on Organic Farms (WWOOF) is an international organization that matches volunteers with host farms. Workers usually are not paid, but they do receive meals and a place to stay. Volunteers, called WWOOFers, are mostly young people eager to experience farm life. Travelers can work their way across countries this way, coming to know places as few tourists will.

than that. Government subsidies, welfare, and off-farm jobs help them make it through winters. Organic farmers tend to do better than conventional ones economically, averaging $26,000 a year.[4]

Job prospects for owner operators are expected to decline about 8 percent from 2008 through 2018, as large companies continue to buy out small farms. In keeping with this trend, jobs for salaried managers are expected to increase about 6 percent. Jobs in service industries such as landscaping are also expected to increase.[5]

On the bright side, small-scale organic agriculture is one of the fastest-growing sectors in the industry. Organic farmers don't buy in bulk like large agribusiness corporations, so they have to pay higher prices for things they need. It might seem impossible for these small farms to compete, but opportunities abound for people willing to exploit niche markets. Farmers with niche markets succeed because they aren't competing with the big corporations directly. For example, an organic farmer might produce specialty items not found elsewhere, such as emu meat.

The biggest barrier to getting into farming is the cost of land. Very large farms that were passed down through family generations have appreciated over time, becoming worth millions of dollars. Most young people entering farming will not be able to buy the land they work, but they may get long-term leases. In another solution, elderly farmers are beginning to partner with young couples who help them work their farms. Many farmers rely on other forms of income in addition to farming.

IMPROVING INCOMES THROUGH DIVERSIFICATION

Organic farmer and author Joel Salatin's farm in Virginia's Shenandoah Valley makes a gross income of approximately $300,000 per year.[6] Polyface Farm is diversified, producing a wide variety of meats, eggs, and sustainable forestry products. What makes his approach to organic farming unique is that Salatin takes advantage of the ways in which his animals work together. For example, he rotates his cows through pastures, and trucks in chickens after the cows. Chickens feast on bugs attracted to the cow manure, getting free food while preventing a pest problem. Clever solutions like this help organic farmers improve their incomes.

A PROFILE OF AN ORGANIC FARMER

Dave Mitchell was a furniture refinisher until the day he saw a strange lump on his hand. It was cancer, caused by years of exposure to thinners and varnishes. The tumor was successfully removed, but his doctor recommended that he quit his job. Organic farming was the healthiest choice Mitchell could think of, but getting land wouldn't be easy.

An open, friendly man, Mitchell is an easy guy to like. That made all the difference when he met a man with land for sale. The two men realized they'd once played on opposing rugby teams, and they soon became friends. Mitchell talked the guy into selling him the land with no bank loan and no interest. He just had to make monthly payments. On a handshake alone, Mitchell became a landowner.

Mitchell hadn't farmed since his boyhood in Oklahoma, and farming is harder in the Rocky Mountains. "In two days, the ground squirrels got all my sugar snap peas," he lamented.[7] Undeterred, he kept on planting. Cold crops like potatoes and greens do best up in the mountains, but that's not all he produces. He also has 60 chickens. "You can't just farm, you got to be diversified!" Mitchell said enthusiastically.[8] He loves his new job, and his harvest is headed for the farmer's market.

Mitchell's advice to young farmers is to avoid debt by taking the time to save for things they need. "And one more thing," he added. "You have to be a steward of the Earth, and the animals."[9]

A DAY IN THE LIFE OF AN ORGANIC FARMER

An organic farmer rises early and heads for the barn to feed the animals. After the barn chores are done, it's time to go out to the fields. The farmer meets his or her employees and starts moving the irrigation pipes to water the fields. Once the water is flowing, it's on to other jobs: weeding, planting seeds, or plowing new fields.

After lunch, the farmer might leave field work to the employees and head into town for a meeting. A restaurant owner wants a regular supply of salad greens, and it's up to the farmer to negotiate a good price. Farmers must do their homework to know exactly what their operating costs are. After all, every successful farmer has a good head for business.

The farmer's work isn't done when evening comes. The animals need evening feedings, and then the office chores begin. That bookkeeping spreadsheet needs updating, and there are always some interesting new farming techniques to read up on. It's a hard life but a happy one, and organic farmers always look forward to tomorrow.

THE LAND LINK PROGRAM

Land Link programs match up older farmers with younger ones, so farms stay under cultivation when their owners retire. Young farmers needing experience may apprentice with the owners and later lease the land. In some cases, the young people eventually buy out the original owners.

A farmer's market is a popular place to find organic produce.

TOP FIVE QUESTIONS ABOUT BECOMING AN ORGANIC FARMER

1. *I want to be a farmer, but I'm not going to inherit land. Is there a way to break into the business if I can't afford to buy a farm?*

   First, learn all you can by volunteering on a farm and growing your own garden. You will definitely want to get certified in permaculture, an organic agriculture system. Once you have a skill set, you can open your own organic landscaping service or other small business. It will take years to save money for a down payment on your farm, but you can do it.

2. *I understand that I need to develop some niche markets if I hope to compete with conventional farmers, but what possibilities are there?*

   Local health food stores often import salad greens from out of state, so that would be a good place to start. Fresh herbs are another good seller; they need to be grown locally, and they bring a good price. Some specialists grow mushrooms, keep honeybees, or raise goats for milk and cheese. There are lots of possibilities.

3. *Do I need to graduate from high school or college in order to be a farmer?*

   Many people without formal educations find jobs on farms. However, you are more likely to make more money with a degree. But your best option is to attend an agricultural college. You could study topics such as genetics, animal breeding, ranch management, horticulture, sheep or cattle production, and dairy or poultry science, among others.

4. *I have a dream of living money-free in the country by raising all my own food. How do I get started?*
   Unfortunately, this isn't a realistic option. Very few people now live a purely subsistence lifestyle, and those who do are members of remote indigenous tribes. In the modern world, land isn't free, and squatters get evicted. Even if you did own land that was paid off, you'd still owe taxes on it. You will need money to buy things you can't make for yourself, and for medical care.

5. *I'm afraid if I go to an agricultural college I will be routed into conventional agriculture. I don't want to abandon my commitment to sustainability. Is there a college that's right for me?*
   Colleges are enthusiastically embracing sustainability; students can now earn master's degrees in the topic. Here are just a few of the many colleges offering programs in organic farming: Washington State University's online Organic Agriculture Certificate, the University of California's Sustainable Agriculture Research Program, and Iowa State University's Organic Agriculture Program.

Organic farmer Joe Hamill produces tomatoes and other crops at his farm in Lavina, Montana.

WOULD YOU MAKE A GOOD ORGANIC FARMER?

So you think you might want to be an organic farmer? Let's look at some of the traits shared by successful farmers and see whether you have them, too. We will start with a really obvious one: do you have a "green thumb"? If your houseplants are thriving so well that your room resembles a rain forest, that's a good sign.

UNDERSTANDING NATURE'S BALANCE

Another important trait shared by organic farmers is perceptiveness. Farmers are keen observers of the natural world, with a good working knowledge of ecology. Understanding the food chain helps them nurture beneficial species and discourage damaging ones. But organic gardening isn't just about plants and bugs. A garden without chemicals is an integral part of the bigger ecosystem around it. Pollinators, birds, reptiles, and even mammals are attracted to organic farms. A healthy ecosystem won't suffer from an overpopulation of any species for long. If one species suddenly increases its numbers, a predator soon shows up to take advantage.

WEASEL IN THE WOODPILE

Becky Elder, owner of the organic landscaping company Blue Planet Earthscapes, has her own wildlife refuge. The National Wildlife Federation certified her Colorado yard as wildlife habitat. Elder never uses poison, so when some mice moved in, she just watched and waited. Soon she spotted an ermine—a tiny white weasel—hunting them. "The weasel was just the size of a hot dog, and the way it moved, it looked like it was swimming the wood pile!" she laughed.[1] When the ermine had eaten all the mice, it moved on. In this suburban garden, nature, not poison, keeps the ecosystem in balance.

You're never too young to learn about growing and selling organic vegetables!

WORKIN' HARD

You might make a good farmer if you love nature and you don't mind physical labor. Most organic farms utilize tractors and other heavy equipment, but there will always be things that need to be done by hand. Getting in there and getting your hands dirty is part of the job, so this occupation is best for strong, healthy people. Those with physical limitations occasionally do still farm, with some accommodations. For example, a farmer with a bad back could have some raised beds built for growing specialty products such as fresh herbs.

ENVIRONMENTALLY AWARE

Do you pay attention to news stories about threatened or endangered animals? Have you researched the dangers of pesticides? If you care about the environment and the health of people around the world, organic farming might be for you. By becoming an organic farmer, you will know you are helping to solve an environmental issue that has plagued the United States for the last several decades. If you want to be part of the solution, organic farming could be your calling.

CHECKLIST

Is organic farming right for you? Take a look at the checklist to see whether this career is a good fit.

- *Are you interested in the natural world?*

- *Do pesticides and other chemicals concern you?*

- *Are you good at fixing things yourself?*

- *Do you enjoy working outside?*

- *Do you like organic foods?*

- *Are you talented at keeping a garden?*

- *Can you live on a tight budget?*

If most of your answers were yes, a job as an organic farmer may be in your future. If you answered no to more of the questions, but you still want to be an organic farmer, don't worry. You can always work hard to develop many of the skills you will need for this career.

HOW TO GET THERE

CLASSES TO TAKE IN HIGH SCHOOL

Future farmers should take biology, environmental science, and chemistry, if their high school offers them. Most high schools don't offer horticulture classes, but you may be able to take one at your local community college. Introductory business and accounting classes are also helpful, especially if you are not planning on taking these classes in college.

Whatever you do, try your best to get good grades. You might not plan on going to college now, but good grades leave you the option of going back later. A low income is fine when you're young and single, but people need more money once they start families. Odds are, even if you farm for a few years, the economic pinch will push you back to college for a degree.

MONEY AND HIGHER EDUCATION

It's time to reflect on the importance money holds for you. Take a moment to envision your ideal adult life. Does it involve new cars, lavish vacations, and private school for your kids? Does it even feature a nice, upper-middle-class house? If so, remember that organic farmers get paid with good times, not good money.

If you've got a yearning for farming, but you like the finer things in life, you can still have it all. You will need to go to a college with an agricultural program, do well, and stick with it all the way to a PhD. A doctorate opens up another employment possibility: research and teaching at a university. Specialists such as geneticists or poultry scientists are still involved in agriculture, but they make much better livings than ordinary farmers. For example, in 2008, the median income for geneticists was $99,572 a year.[2] However, these specialist jobs differ greatly from being an organic farmer.

Still determined to farm? In that case, the most important thing you can do is to get certified in permaculture. Think of permaculture as higher education for organic farmers. Courses can be completed in as little as two weeks, and the knowledge you will gain will be worth the investment in tuition. You can even get certified to teach the subject and make a

WHAT'S PERMACULTURE?

In a permaculture course, you will learn how to create a garden that mimics a natural forest. Natural forests grow in layers, with tall trees towering over smaller trees and bushes, which shelter a low-growing herb layer. Root vegetables make use of underground space, too. Permaculture gardens are some of the most productive in the world because they're three-dimensional. The tall trees produce fruit, nuts, or wood. The bushes bear fruit, and vegetables grow in sunny patches throughout.

Mixing species is also a great strategy for foiling insect pests. If plants of one kind are together, insect pests can find one kind they like and wipe it out.

modest living organizing and teaching permaculture design courses.

NETWORKING

Networking is important in farming, just as it is in any business. Visit farmer's markets, and meet the locals. You should also get to know the businesspeople in your town, even if they're not farmers. One of them might turn out to be your best customer some day. Clubs and organizations are another fun way to connect with fellow plant lovers. Permaculture courses spawn close-knit communities, as do 4-H and Future Farmers of America (FFA) clubs. These clubs can teach you about farming and even give you hands-on farming experience. If you can't find these clubs, any gardening club will do.

JOIN 4-H

4-H is more than a club for young people. It's a fun way to learn leadership and practical skills. The organization began in rural areas, when agricultural researchers found that conservative older farmers wouldn't adopt new methods. Teaching young people was the answer. Kids did individual projects that put new ideas into practice, and then they taught their parents. Now 4-H clubs can be found in cities, too. Each local group has a focus, such as agriculture, science and technology, or health.

Members of the Future Farmers of America get hands-on experience with farm animals.

Conservationist Dr. Iain Douglas-Hamilton, founder of
Save the Elephants, is pictured with a 43-year-old
elephant at the Indianapolis Zoo.

WHAT IS A PROFESSIONAL CONSERVATIONIST?

Professional conservationists get paid to do some
of the most important work there is—to save life
on Earth. We are now in the midst of the greatest mass
extinction since the dinosaurs died out 65 million years ago.

Some scientists believe that what makes this mass extinction different is that humans are contributing to it. The human population is growing rapidly, especially in developing nations. Species such as pigeons and rats can share space with humans, but most others cannot. When we move in, they die out.

Why should we care if some obscure bug or plant disappears, or even if whole forests are razed? There are two main reasons to care. First is the value inherent in every life form. Conservationists believe that even if there is no seemingly practical use for a creature, it still has the right to exist. The second reason is a purely selfish one: we need intact ecosystems to survive for our own livelihood. This might not be immediately obvious, but ecologies are networks made up of relationships among species. When enough species disappear, the entire ecosystem collapses. Don't forget that humans, our livestock, and our crops are part of this same ecosystem.

FIVE WAYS TO HELP THE PLANET

1. Eat local—grow your own food or buy food from local farmers.

2. Weed the dandelions in your lawn by hand rather than poisoning them.

3. Eat less meat.

4. Avoid buying new things. Buy used ones or just reuse what you have.

5. Don't own a car. Seek other modes of transportation.

WANT TO BE A LOBBYIST?

Are you charming, persuasive, and passionate about politics? If so, you might make a good lobbyist. Young want-to-be lobbyists should start by getting internships as congressional aides, in government agencies, or in lobbying firms. There are no college majors in lobbying and no necessary certifications. Lobbyists only have to register with state and federal governments. Retired politicians often leverage their influence as lobbyists, but there are still openings for interested young people.

Professional conservationists save species, prevent pollution, and plan for a better future. They do some of the most important work on Earth.

How do you become a professional conservationist? Who would hire you if you did? The number of opportunities may surprise you. Conservationists work for universities, nonprofit organizations, governments, zoos, and nature centers. A few even create their own jobs by becoming authors, photographers, or filmmakers.

The most obvious path to becoming a professional conservationist is to get a degree in conservation biology or environmental science, but that's not the only approach. Conservation organizations do need staff scientists, but they also hire specialists in human resources, finance, legal services, technology, marketing, and membership. Nonprofit organizations also rely on grant writers, event planners, lobbyists, and volunteer coordinators. Grant writing is a very useful skill for a conservationist. Governments also hire conservation scientists such as biologists, foresters, range managers, and soil conservationists, among others. In a sense, all of these people are professional conservationists, but here we will focus on one: staffer at an environmental organization.

WHAT IS A PROFESSIONAL CONSERVATIONIST'S WORK ENVIRONMENT?

The main offices of many conservation organizations are located in Washington DC, so staffers live urban lifestyles. Most work is done from offices, either on a computer or telephone, with breaks for meetings with lawmakers, colleagues, and supporters. Conservation organizations tend to be progressive in their office management policies, with some even offering employees eco-perks such as free use of bicycles.

HOW IS THE JOB MARKET FOR PROFESSIONAL CONSERVATIONISTS?

Jobs for conservation scientists are expected to increase about 12 percent by 2018, mostly as a result of hiring by federal, state, and local governments.[1] Western forests have continuing issues with fire management and pine beetle infestation, so experts in those specialties will be in demand.

In good news for job seekers, conservation organizations are doing well despite the sluggish economy. In 2009, donations were up 2.7 percent, to an impressive $6.2 billion total.[2] In 2010, the disastrous oil spill in the Gulf of Mexico appeared to increase the number of donations.

"The oil spill has taken environmental consciousness up five notches," said Rob Moher, vice president for development and marketing at the Conservancy of Southwest Florida. "Everybody is thinking about how delicate and vulnerable and connected things are. And we're saying that along with all the critical work we do every day for our estuaries and wildlife and sea turtles, we all have to be ready for this and for the next crisis."[3]

A PROFILE OF A PROFESSIONAL CONSERVATIONIST

Irene Jones has a bachelor's degree in biology, but she always knew she wanted to work on real-world policy issues. That's what she does as a staff member at the Friends of the Mississippi River (FMR), a citizen organization concerned with the health of the Mississippi River in the Twin Cities area of Minnesota. The Mississippi River needs friends; it has water-quality problems, and developers covet the remaining open land along its banks.

Conservation work can become a series of responses to one crisis after another, leaving activists little time to work on long-term solutions. The FMR faced this challenge for years as they fought one proposed riverbank development after another. "I was banging my head against the wall trying to get local issues to go the way I wanted them to," Jones recalled. "We would gather information, meet with citizens,

The Friends of the Mississippi River is a conservation group that works to preserve the health of the Mississippi River in the Twin Cities area.

and make our case. It was a long, painful process. I felt like I kept fighting the same fight over and over."[4]

Finally, in 2009, a critical piece of FMR-backed legislation passed, and the Mississippi River Critical Area was protected. "It was a huge victory," Jones said with satisfaction.[5]

Villagers in Cameroon in western Africa plant rain forest plants as part of a conservation effort.

Are you looking forward to a career in conservation? Jones has some advice for you. "Get politically involved in your community. It's a great way to get to know people who can help you later in your policy career."[6]

A DAY IN THE LIFE OF A PROFESSIONAL CONSERVATIONIST

A typical environmental advocate does a lot of writing, including grant proposals, press releases, blogs, and letters to politicians or supporters. Every day, there are meetings to attend, as staffers gather to respond to a crisis or draft strategies. Donor relations are crucial, so planners stage frequent entertaining and educational events for their supporters. Staffers regularly attend these after-hours events.

FRUSTRATION AND BURNOUT

Just about every environmental activist has suffered from burnout at one point or another. Some dedicated volunteers exhaust themselves by attending meetings practically every night of the week. To combat burnout among core volunteers, environmental groups need to recruit new members and encourage them to take on responsibilities.

TOP FIVE QUESTIONS ABOUT BECOMING A PROFESSIONAL CONSERVATIONIST

1. *Besides going to college, what's the most important thing I can do to prepare for a job in environmental advocacy?*
   Develop your leadership skills. You might volunteer to lead educational programs at your local nature center or intern at an environmental organization. It will look good on your resume, too!

2. *I'd love to work for an environmental organization, but I'm confused about the term* nonprofit. *Does this mean that nonprofit organizations rely only on volunteers?*
   No, employees of nonprofit organizations are paid, sometimes quite well. Nonprofit organizations are called "nonprofit" because they don't distribute excess funds to shareholders or other owners. Nonprofits are required to use these monies to further their charitable, educational, or recreational goals.

3. *My goal is to eventually run a national environmental organization. What should I major in when I go to college?*
   Environmental advocacy majors are offered at select colleges, but a history of activism and leadership in environmental organizations is more important than your major. Sierra Club President Robin Mann has master's degrees in economics and international

relations. Natural Resource Defense Council (NRDC) President Frances Beinecke chose environmental studies. Mark Tercek, president and CEO of the Nature Conservancy, has a background in business and finance. Whichever major you choose, you will need a college degree and probably graduate school to compete for top jobs.

4. *I have a history of civil disobedience for environmental causes. I've been arrested twice at protests. Will this affect my chances of getting hired by an environmental organization?*
    The environmental community is split on this issue. Some organizations are strictly law-abiding, while others insist on breaking the law only if it is unjust, but always doing it in a nonviolent manner. Even Gandhi broke the law, so if your arrests were for nonviolent protest—not ecoterrorism—you will probably be fine.

5. *What's a typical entry-level salary for an environmental advocate?*
    Environmental advocates typically earn between $19,000 and $50,000 per year, but you can expect to start on the low end.[7]

A baby great horned owl is pictured at the Blandford Nature Center in Grand Rapids, Michigan. Many conservationists find jobs at nature centers and zoos.

WOULD YOU MAKE A GOOD PROFESSIONAL CONSERVATIONIST?

Does a career as a professional conservationist sound interesting to you? Many conservationists would say they love their jobs but find them pretty demanding. Do you have the determination and skills to enter this field? If so, you could be on your way to your dream job!

TEAM PLAYER

Perhaps the most important trait of a successful conservationist is the ability to be an effective team member. The skill set of a conservationist is essentially that of a politician, and team members must be able to act as either leaders or followers as the occasion demands. A facility for reaching consensus in groups is vital. Activists who don't handle compromise well can risk frustration and burnout.

CONFLICT RESOLUTION

One key issue with group dynamics is conflict resolution. Wherever there are humans in groups, there will be disagreements. No matter how committed the members are to their cause, infighting can tear groups apart. Tact and good humor can go a long way toward making your group an effective one.

WRITING AND PUBLIC SPEAKING SKILLS

Communication is another talent shared by effective environmentalists. If you become a professional conservationist, you will spend much of your time writing, so learn how to do it quickly and well. Public speaking is another way for a newcomer to stand out. Every conservation organization has its public speakers, but they usually don't

Dead pogies float in a fish kill on the Louisiana coast in September 2010 after the Gulf of Mexico oil spill. Conservationists try to prevent disasters like this one.

have many. Most people aren't good at public speaking and may flatly refuse to do it at all. In one survey, the fear of public speaking ranked higher than the fear of death.[1] Knowing this now gives you an advantage. You might not be a good speaker yet, but you can become one. Activists who are gifted orators often find themselves vaulted to positions of prominence in their organizations.

CHECKLIST

Have you got what it takes to become a professional conservationist? Review the checklist below, and find out.

- *Have you ever been involved in a protest or a rally?*

- *Do you enjoy nature, and do you want to preserve it?*

- *Are you concerned about issues such as pollution, pesticide use, climate change, and endangered species?*

- *Are you good at resolving conflicts and compromising with your opponents?*

- *Are you interested in law and politics?*

- *Do you feel passionately about your positions on environmental issues?*

- *Are you a good communicator?*

If you answered yes to most of these questions, you would probably make a great conservationist. But don't worry if you answered no to some answers, too. With enough determination and willingness to learn, you can still take on this career.

HOW TO GET THERE

CLASSES TO TAKE

Still interested in becoming a professional conservationist? Then let's look at the classes you will want to take in high school. Remember that you can get into conservation from a lot of different angles, so you're not limited there. Whatever your strengths are, you still want to understand how ecosystems work, so get the best grasp of biology and ecology that you can. Take environmental science if it's offered, as well as statistics. Math has its place in the study of ecology, so tackle calculus if possible. You already know that conservationists are communicators, so hit those English and public-speaking classes hard, too.

In college, you should start thinking about your future specialty. Will you be a staff scientist at an environmental organization?

GREENPEACE AND SEA SHEPHERD CONSERVATION SOCIETY

Sometimes organizations with the same goals differ about their methods. Greenpeace and Sea Shepherd Conservation Society both say they act nonviolently to save whales, but they disagree about what constitutes violence. Neither organization has ever harmed a person, but a Sea Shepherd ship has rammed whaling ships and sunk unmanned whaling vessels in port. Greenpeace opposes these forceful tactics. Instead, they fly protest banners and launch small boats that get between whalers and whales. In an official press release, Greenpeace states, "We passionately want to stop whaling, and will do so peacefully. That's why we won't help Sea Shepherd."[2]

"When Greenpeace shows up in Antarctica, they film whaling and buzz the whalers in inflatable boats," counters Sea Shepherd Captain Paul Watson. "The whalers simply continue whaling, looking at Greenpeacers as a minor annoyance. When Sea Shepherd ships show up, the whalers stop the killing and they run."[3]

Or would you rather work there as a political expert, financial wizard, marketing manager, or grant writer? Unless you know exactly how you want to fit in, a major in environmental studies is a good choice. As an undergraduate in environmental studies, you will develop a strong background in ecological and physical sciences, and then you will apply that knowledge to solving environmental problems. Environmental studies programs specifically prepare students for leadership positions in environmental organizations, but you can also use them as springboards into graduate school.

INTERNSHIPS AND NETWORKING

Some of your most important learning will occur outside of class. If you're serious about a career as a conservationist, get in as much volunteer time as you can. Watch how the most effective activists work, and don't be afraid to ask questions. People are usually happy to share what they know. If an organization isn't all you hoped it would be, move on. Seeing a variety of groups is a plus at this stage. You will quickly become savvy at spotting dysfunctional groups and picking out the good ones, too.

LETTERS OF RECOMMENDATION

Keep in touch with the professionals whom you respect, and cultivate them as mentors. Remember that, in most cases, you will need at least two letters of recommendation to get into college, and three more if you apply for graduate school. Forging relationships early ensures that your mentors will be able to write strong letters for you—letters praising your

ASSERTIVENESS TRAINING

Activists have to be willing to confront their opponents, whether those opponents are individual polluters or irresponsible corporations. Confrontation is very difficult for many people, and the anxiety it provokes may paralyze an otherwise committed conservationist. If this sounds familiar to you, then you may benefit from assertiveness training. Assertiveness training helps passive people become self-confident, not aggressive or domineering. Think of people like Martin Luther King Jr. and Mahatma Gandhi. Despite their nonviolent tactics, they stood up assertively for their beliefs.

years of volunteer work and all your outstanding accomplishments. Without a mentor, you will just be one of the thousands of applicants with letters saying you took some teacher's class, and you got an A. Which recommendation would you rather have?

Science and math classes are important for students interested in conservation.

Posters display Washington DC-area buildings that were to be retrofitted with new energy-saving technology.

WHAT IS AN ALTERNATIVE ENERGY EXPERT?

Pollution, climate change, and declining oil and natural gas supplies have left energy experts looking for alternatives to fossil fuels. Currently, no single alternative can replace fossil fuels, but fossil fuels won't last forever. As supplies decline, alternative energies must take on a greater role. Federal tax credits have started to make energy efficiency more attainable. According to the US Bureau of Labor Statistics, renewable energy industry is growing faster than any other part of the electric power industry.

PEAK OIL

Peak oil activists tell us that global oil production peaked back in 2005 and is now declining. These activists are right to be concerned, but declining oil supplies won't mean empty gas pumps any time soon. Global oil production has increased gradually since the 1930s. Even if the touted 2005 peak turns out to be correct, it's still a long, gradual slope back down to zero.[1] You will probably see fossil fuels in use for the rest of your life, but the easy-to-reach sources are running out. Remaining supplies are under deep seafloors and in other difficult places, so prices will probably increase faster than supplies will run out.

The smart thing to do would be to stop depending on oil before the situation becomes critical, and alternative energy experts are helping us to do that. Want to jump on board? There are many opportunities. First, let's look over your job possibilities in the solar power industry.

- *Solar Engineer:* The leaders of the solar power industry are the engineers who invent and develop new solar energy systems. Since colleges are still developing degree programs in solar energy, today's professionals tend to be physicists or electrical engineers. They

NOT-SO-GREEN ALTERNATIVE ENERGIES

Biofuels and hydroelectric and nuclear power are, technically, alternative energies since they're not fossil fuel based. So, why aren't they considered clean and green energy alternatives? They're all environmentally damaging in different ways. Biofuels include ethanol made from corn and biodiesel made from vegetable oil, so they're plant based. But biofuels still have to be burned, and they cause pollution just like fossil fuels do. They also raise a social concern: Are we diverting food from the poor to make fuel?

Hydroelectric and nuclear power don't create air pollution, so in that sense they are cleaner than fossil fuels. But nuclear power plants create radioactive waste, and the dams needed for hydroelectric power keep fish from reaching their spawning grounds. That's why biofuels, hydroelectric power, and nuclear power are in the not-so-green group of alternative energies.

work at universities, research labs, and on solar power "farms."

• *Solar Installer:* Individuals in this entry-level position mount solar panels and connect them to a building's wiring. The need for safe handling of electricity led to a national certification program by the North American Board of Certified Energy Practitioners (NABCEP).

• *Solar Technician:* Solar technicians inspect, repair, and may install solar panel systems. Most techs learn on the job rather than at universities, but they may still test for certification.

WHAT ABOUT WIND?

A 2008 report from the US Department of Energy inspired wind industry promoters and environmentalists alike. "The report shows that wind power can provide 20 percent of the nation's electricity by 2030, and be a critical part of the solution to global warming. This level of wind power is the equivalent of taking 140 million cars off the road," explained American Wind Energy Association Executive Director, Randall Swisher.[2]

Although some homes do rely on small wind generators for electricity, it's the large wind farms that are really making the news. Currently, the world's largest land-based wind farm is a 47,000-acre (19,020-ha) spread in Texas that powers 220,000 homes.[3] Even larger ones are on the way. The newest trend is to build wind farms offshore to take advantage of the strong, steady ocean winds. Construction plans mean jobs. Here are some upcoming opportunities in the wind energy industry:

- *Manufacturing:* Producing turbines, towers, and gearboxes

- *Sales and Marketing:* Connecting with customers who want large or small turbines

- *Service:* Development, transportation, turbine technicians

Solar and wind power are the best known types of renewable energy, but other sources are under development. Geothermal energy and tide power are the most promising.

An solar technician repairs a solar panel.

WHAT IS AN ALTERNATIVE ENERGY EXPERT'S WORK ENVIRONMENT?

Work environments vary at each level of the industry. Technicians who perform installation and repairs will mostly work outside, meeting with customers at job sites. People who are afraid of heights may want to think twice before becoming alternative energy technicians. Wind turbines soar approximately 230 feet (70.1 m) high, and techs, roped in for safety, have to get up there and make repairs.[4] Solar panel installers have it easier. Most of them only need to climb up on residential roofs.

Renewable energy engineers spend more of their time in offices, although they will go out to inspect equipment from time to time. They also spend at least half of each day attending meetings and doing paperwork.

HOW IS THE JOB MARKET FOR ALTERNATIVE ENERGY EXPERTS?

As of 2009, the renewable energy industry was growing three times as fast as the US economy as a whole, increasing 25 percent per year. In 2007, the United States had 9 million jobs in renewable energy and energy efficiency. By 2030, the country could have up to 37 million green energy jobs.[5]

Despite these glowing predictions, many small solar and wind energy businesses are struggling. These businesses rely on residential customers who want to add solar panels or build off-grid homes that don't rely on the power company. The economic downturn has caused most of these customers to rethink big expenditures. As a result, most job growth is expected in large commercial wind farms.

A PROFILE OF AN ALTERNATIVE ENERGY EXPERT

As a student, Jerrolynn Kawamoto didn't plan on becoming a green energy expert. She focused on science, earning a PhD in anatomy. It wasn't until many years later that she became the system designer and project manager at RPM Renewable in Woodland Park, Colorado.

"Most of my education isn't relevant now," Kawamoto says, but the work ethic that got her through her PhD sure is.[6]

Her job at RPM Renewable requires her to stay up to date on the latest technology, learning the material and then training company technicians.

On a typical day, she might meet with customers and do a site analysis on their property. A site analysis involves more than seeing whether a roof is strong and sunny enough for solar panels. Before installing, she also has to make sure the customers are in compliance with the regulations of homeowners' associations, counties, and utility companies.

Thinking about starting your own renewable energy business? "Get lots of financing," Kawamoto advises. "Plan to be in business for one year before you make any money."[7] The main stumbling block in small-scale renewable energy is the high initial investment for customers, even with existing tax credits and utility payback programs. That's why Kawamoto advises young designers to charge up-front for their design work. "Designs are time-consuming, so I charge 10 percent of the cost of the system for the design."[8] That initial investment encourages customers to see the process through.

The way Kawamoto sees it, investing in

SELL ENERGY TO YOUR UTILITY COMPANY

The Public Utility Regulatory Policies Act (PURPA) of 1978 requires utility companies to buy back energy that consumers put back into the grid, or power system, via renewable energy. Payback rates are based on the cost of the company generating the electricity or buying it from another utility.

Seth Stanfield, wind plant supervisor, looks over the machinery in the wind turbine cell at the PPM Energy wind farm in Wasco, Oregon.

renewable energy is the most important thing our society can do. "It will help individuals to keep costs down, and it will help the planet, too."[9]

A DAY IN THE LIFE OF AN ALTERNATIVE ENERGY EXPERT

Someone who opens a small renewable energy business will spend part of each day sorting through messages from potential clients. To be financially successful, the business owner will need to quickly separate serious buyers from interested people who are only dreaming. Environmentally minded people will often call to ask questions, but customers whose homes already rely on conventional power sources are unlikely to make large investments. The energy expert needs to be congenial enough to make a good impression without wasting too much time in unprofitable conversations.

The energy expert meets with serious customers in person to hear their needs before designing a system for them. After these meetings, the expert will get a tour of the clients' property and do a site analysis. If all goes well, the energy expert will soon be designing and installing a system sized to meet their needs. Depending on how busy the business owner is, some design work might be done at home, after hours. Many business owners hire installers to do all the installations, but smaller operators work right alongside their employees.

On slower days, savvy business owners check in with former clients to see whether the systems are meeting their needs. Good customer service improves the energy expert's reputation and ensures clients will refer the expert to others.

Wind turbines are a growing source of green energy
in the United States.

TOP FIVE QUESTIONS ABOUT BECOMING AN ALTERNATIVE ENERGY EXPERT

1. *What kind of training will I need to become a solar installer?*

    Your first step would be to take the North American Board of Certified Energy Practitioners (NABCEP) Entry Level Course to prepare you for the NABCEP PV Entry Level Exam. You can later pass a higher-level exam to become a NABCEP Certified PV Installer. NABCEP certifications are not government-issued licenses, so you still need to comply with local licensing requirements. Incidentally, similar courses and certificates exist for small wind installers.

2. *Are there scholarships available to help students pay for renewable energy training programs?*

    Yes, Solar Energy International (SEI) is one of many organizations that offer scholarships in renewable energy technology and sustainable design. Larger colleges and universities often have sustainability programs, too, and they always offer scholarships, financial aid, and work study to defray costs.

3. *What kind of salary can I expect as a solar installer? What if I specialize in wind generator installation instead?*
   As a solar installer you will probably make about $25,000 to $75,000 a year.[10] If you specialize in installation and maintenance of wind generators, you might make more. Average salary for wind techs is approximately $48,000 a year, with higher salaries in cities where the cost of living is high.[11]

4. *Do I need to be a certified electrician to work with solar energy?*
   A solar installer can install solar panels. Only a certified electrician may legally hook up solar panels to the home's electrical wiring. The minute a panel is hooked up to the home's wiring it is live, so amateur installers risk electrocution.

5. *If I got a degree as a renewable energy systems designer, how would my income compare to a technician's?*
   Your income as a designer would generally be higher than a technician's income. But how much higher depends on what kind of energy system you design and where you work.

Wind turbine technicians are not afraid to climb
260-foot (79-m) towers!

WOULD YOU MAKE A GOOD ALTERNATIVE ENERGY EXPERT?

I f a career as an alternative energy expert interests you, there are some basic skills that you will want to have. Not everyone is suited for every career. Find out whether this job is your match!

UNDERSTANDING OF MECHANICS

Whether they earned a certificate or a college degree, successful alternative energy experts tend to share similar interests and skills. The most important of these is mechanical aptitude. If you enjoy machines and are curious about how things work, this might be the career for you. Math skills help, too, because math is a prerequisite for most engineering courses.

PEOPLE SKILLS

Both technicians and engineers will spend time with customers and colleagues, so people skills are important. This can be a challenge for technical types. "Poor communication has been such a blocker to the careers of many engineers I've managed and mentored," says Microsoft development manager Philip Su.[1]

ENERGY FROM WAVES AND TIDES

Another possible career path for renewable energy engineers is to research tidal or wave power generation. Currently, the world's only tidal power station is in France. It uses the power of tide-driven ocean water entering and leaving a tidal basin to run conventional hydroelectric turbines. This station generates clean energy, but the sediment buildup behind the dam is bad for marine life.

Wave power is a newer and greener possibility. Most wave power generators are very small-scale, but they have been used to power small lighthouses. Can this technology be scaled up to provide significant amounts of energy? Join the research team and find out.

Su says that extroverts can help. They can draw out their introverted colleagues in one-on-one conversations or via e-mailed follow-ups after meetings. "The goal shouldn't be to change an introvert into an extrovert. Instead, it's to make both introverts and extroverts better communicators."[2]

What can you do if you're an introvert? Make an effort to talk to people you don't know, even if it comes off sounding a little scripted at first. If you often find yourself tongue-tied in a group of classmates, it doesn't hurt to plan a few conversation starters ahead of time. For example, you might make it a habit to attend local concerts or shows. It's easy to start conversations by asking whether people were there, or what they thought of the event. With effort, you can develop great social skills.

BEYOND SOLAR AND WIND

Renewables aren't limited to solar and wind power. Geothermal energy—heat or steam from inside the earth—can be harnessed to provide heat and electricity, too. One geothermal heat pump design has a deep vertical pipe full of circulating water or coolant that absorbs heat underground and then brings it up. Drilling is a significant cost, and systems that circulate liquids use electricity to operate the pumps. Even with these costs, geothermal systems still use 25 to 50 percent less energy than conventional furnaces.[3]

Geothermal power plants are already operating in some areas, but the technology is new to residential customers. Students who become experts in residential geothermal systems could be on the cutting edge of a new industry.

Geothermal power stations convert heat
from the earth into electricity.

CHECKLIST

Got the right stuff to be an alternative energy expert? Take a
look at this checklist and find out.

- *Do you care about the environment, and do you want to
  encourage the use of alternative energies?*

- *Do you enjoy mechanics, science, and math classes?*

- *Are you exacting and careful with details?*

- *Do you enjoy using new computers and other electronic
  gadgets?*

- *Do you like the challenge of putting things together?*

*If you answered yes to most of these questions, you would
probably make a good alternative energy expert. Still,*

remember that even if you don't have all of these skills and interests, you can still enter the field if you are determined to succeed.

HOW TO GET THERE

CLASSES TO TAKE IN HIGH SCHOOL

In high school, take math as far as you can, all the way through calculus if possible. Add physics and chemistry, and take industrial tech, or shop, class, too, if your school offers it. Here's a surprise: you might not like communications classes, but you will need them. Remember that alternative energy experts spend a good portion of their day doing paperwork and meeting with colleagues and clients.

The nice thing about the renewable energy industry is that both average students and high-achieving ones can find places there. It will take top grades to get into an engineering program, but average students can still find jobs in the industry as technicians.

SHOULD I MAJOR IN RENEWABLE ENERGY ENGINEERING?

The wind and solar power industries have worked with a few select colleges to develop programs in renewable energy engineering. One example is the bachelor's of science in Renewable Energy Engineering offered by the Oregon Institute of Technology. The program begins with chemistry, physics, and mathematics, but advanced students take courses in subjects such as photovoltaics (PV), wind power, and renewable energy transportation systems.

Community colleges also offer two-year degree programs and one-year certificates in renewable energy design and installation. In the shorter programs, students go directly into classes such as PV and solar home design. They will graduate ready to be hired as technicians or start their own small businesses doing residential solar panel installation. At the lowest level of the industry are the entry-level employees with no degrees or certificates. They get on-the-job training but are unlikely to rise very far in any company.

RENEWABLE ENERGY DESIGN OR ENGINEERING?

Renewable energy design is different from renewable energy engineering. Design experts can choose the best system for a particular home or business. Engineering experts have more education, so they understand the nuts and bolts of the systems and the theories behind them, and they may even invent new systems.

As always, people who get advanced degrees will take longer to get out into the workforce, but they will make more money once they get there. The best way to decide which approach is right for you is to honestly evaluate your strengths and weaknesses as well as your current economic situation. Are you a strong student, or do you struggle? Do you need to support yourself soon, or will parental or scholarship support help you get through college?

NETWORKING

No matter which industry you're interested in, networking is important. Students can learn a lot by participating in networking groups online, but you also need to get out and meet real people. One way that young people can break in is by getting entry-level jobs as part-time installers. However, anyone under the age of 18 is prohibited from being employed in hazardous jobs, including those that require work on a roof. Outside the classroom, learn all you can by reading voraciously. Studying up on an industry can help you decide which career is really for you.

Workers install solar panels.

GET YOUR FOOT IN THE DOOR

Now that you have a sense of what career you're interested in, it's time to do some job shadowing, rock that interview, and land the job. For now, the "job" might be an unpaid internship or volunteer opportunity, but those are important stepping stones to success. They might even lead to a full-time position in the future. Take them as seriously as you would a real job.

Start learning about the green industry now. Explore the career that interests you most, but also stay open to other possibilities. The more you know about the industry, the easier it will be for you to make contacts with professionals in the field—a key step toward getting the job.

The first step is to start making contacts in professional organizations. Practice your "elevator speech"—that 30-second introduction of yourself and your career goals—so you will sound polished when you get on the phone. A good place to start is by asking whether organization members would allow you to "shadow" them for a day. Shadowing just involves following someone around for a day so you can see what his or her job is like. It's also a great way to make contacts.

Another option for students who don't have a whole day to spend is to request an informational meeting with a member of an organization. Try to find out who a few of the members are before making the call. It's more effective to request a particular person than to ask for a random member who would like to meet with a student.

Once you have made some contacts in the field, it is a good idea to start looking for an internship or an entry-level job in the industry. Your contacts might be able to keep an eye out for some opportunities for you. These opportunities can give you a first-hand look at what your career would be like in the green industry. This can help you decide if this is the field for you.

When you choose whether to continue your education after high school, think about your career and personal goals first. Does your career of choice require a college degree? If so, what colleges offer majors in the subject? If not, would you be disappointed if you did not attend college? How might a college degree help you if you decide to change careers later? Be sure to seek advice from guidance and career counselors as well as the contacts you have made in the industry. Look at all your options before making a final decision about your education.

Stay determined and informed. Keep your eyes open for new ways to increase your experience in the field. Before you know it, you will have the skills and experience to land a green job!

PROFESSIONAL ORGANIZATIONS

Here are some professional organizations you might want to contact for more information about the jobs in this book.

GREEN ARCHITECT

American Institute of Architects
www.aia.org

The Royal Architectural Institute of Canada
www.raic.org

US Green Building Council
www.usgbc.org

ORGANIC FARMER

International Federation of Organic Agriculture Movements
www.ifoam.org

Organic Consumers Association
www.organicconsumers.org

Organic Farming Research Association
www.ofrf.org

Organic Trade Association
www.ota.com

PROFESSIONAL CONSERVATIONIST

The Ecological Society of America
www.esa.org

Environmental Law Alliance Worldwide
www.elaw.org

Society for Conservation Biology
www.conbio.org

Soil and Water Conservation Society
www.swcs.org

ALTERNATIVE ENERGY EXPERT

The American Council on Renewable Energy
www.acore.org

American Solar Energy Society
www.ases.org

American Wind Energy Association
www.awea.org

Canadian Renewable Fuels Association
www.greenfuels.org

MARKET FACTS

JOB	NUMBER OF JOBS	GROWTH RATE	
Architect	101,000	faster than average	
Farmer	986,000	decline moderately, but organic farmers may do better	
Professional Conservationist	16,810	as fast as average	
Alternative Energy Jobs	9 million	faster than average	

	ANNUAL MEDIAN WAGE	RELATED JOBS	SKILLS
	$72,000	landscape architect, interior designer, green builder/ contractor	artistic, visual-spatial learner, math oriented, environmentally conscious
	$32,350	green landscaping, organic gardening service, horticulture	hard worker, understanding of nature, handy
	$60,160	biologist, ranch manager, lobbyist	confident, good communicator, diplomatic, passionate
	dependent on position	geothermal engineering, wave power engineering	technical, math and science minded, environmentally conscious

All statistics from the *Bureau of Labor Statistics Occupational Outlook Handbook, 2010–2011 Edition* and the American Solar Energy Society

GLOSSARY

aesthetic
Having to do with art, beauty, or appearance.

alternative energies
Energies not derived from fossil fuels.

carcinogens
Chemicals known to cause cancer.

colleagues
People who are members of one's profession.

consensus
Agreement reached by a group as a majority.

conventional
According to the usual method of production; used in contrast to green or environmentally friendly production methods.

dysfunctional
Incorrect or abnormal, as related to social functioning.

embodied energy
The energy needed to acquire, manufacture, and transport a building material.

genetically modified
When something's genetic material has been altered in a way that does not occur naturally.

invisible structures
Cultural and financial practices that affect the environment.

mass extinction
A process in which huge numbers of species die out suddenly.

mechanical aptitude
A natural ability to perform mechanical tasks and understand the workings of machines.

mentor
A person who serves as a teacher or a trusted counselor.

outgas
The slow release of a usually toxic gas contained in a building material.

phthalates
Toxic chemicals used to make plastics pliable.

sustainable
A way of life in which human needs are met without diminishing the ability of other people, wild species, or future generations to survive.

ADDITIONAL RESOURCES

FURTHER READINGS

Cassio, Jim, and Alice Rush. *Green Careers: Choosing Work for a Sustainable Future.* Gabriola Island, B.C., Canada: New Society, 2009. Print.

Deitche, Scott. *Green Collar Jobs: Environmental Careers for the 21st Century.* Santa Barbara, CA: Praeger, 2010. Print.

Lechner, Norbert. *Heating, Cooling, Lighting: Sustainable Design Methods for Architects.* Danvers, MA: Wiley, 2009. Print.

Llewellyn, Bronwyn. *A Guide to Eco-Friendly Employment.* Avon, MA: F + W, 2008. Print.

McClelland, Carol L. *Green Careers for Dummies.* Hoboken, NJ: Wiley, 2010. Print.

McNamee, Gregory. *Careers in Renewable Energy: Get a Green Energy Job.* Masonville, CO: PixyJack, 2008. Print.

Pitman, Dick. *A Wild Life: Adventures of an Accidental Conservationist in Africa.* Guilford, CT: Globe Pequot, 2008. Print.

Sanders, Scott Russell. *A Conservationist Manifesto*. Bloomington, IN: Indiana University Press, 2009. Print.

Wiswall, Richard. *The Organic Farmers Business Handbook*. White River Junction, VT: Chelsea Green, 2009. Print.

WEB LINKS

To learn more about green jobs, visit ABDO Publishing Company online at **www.abdopublishing.com**. Web sites about green jobs are featured on our Book Links page. These links are routinely monitored and updated to provide the most current information available.

SOURCE NOTES

CHAPTER 1. IS A GREEN JOB FOR YOU?

1. Green Inaugural Ball. *Live Earth*. Live Earth, 20 Jan. 2010. Web. 15 July 2010.

2. Joubert, Derek and Beverly. "Interview with Boyd Matson." *National Geographic Events: Speakers Bureau*. National Geographic Society, n.d. Web. 20 Sept. 2010.

3. Britta Belli, Kathryn Gutlebar, Julia Hirsch, Jesica Knoblauch, and Shawn Query. "10 Great Green Opportunities." *Emagazine.com*. E - The Environmental Magazine, Nov./Dec. 2007. Web. 15 July 2010.

CHAPTER 2. WHAT IS A GREEN ARCHITECT?

1. U.S. Bureau of Labor Statistics. "Occupational Employment and Wages, May 2009: Architects, Except Landscape and Naval." *Occupational Outlook Handbook, 2010-11 Edition*. U.S. Bureau of Labor Statistics, 14 May 2010. Web. 21 Sept. 2010.

2. "Quick Facts on Nontraditional Occupations for Women." *Women's Bureau*. U.S. Department of Labor, Apr. 2008. Web. 21 Sept. 2010.

3. Brentin Mock. "Blacklisted." *americancity.org*. Next American City, 2008 Web. 21 Sept. 2010.

4. U.S. Bureau of Labor Statistics. "Architects, Except Landscape and Naval." *Occupational Outlook Handbook, 2010-11 Edition*. U.S. Bureau of Labor Statistics, 17 Dec. 2009. Web. 15 July 2010.

5. Jeanne Sahadi. "Personal Finance: Big jobs that Pay Badly." *CNNMoney.com*. Cable News Network, 17 Aug. 2005. Web. 15 July 2010.

6. Derek Trost. Message to the author. 14 July 2010. E-mail.

7. Ibid.

8. Ibid.

9. Ibid.

10. Ibid.

CHAPTER 3. WOULD YOU MAKE A GOOD GREEN ARCHITECT?

1. Richard Meier. "Is Architecture Art?" *Big Think*. n.p. 4 Feb. 2008. Web. 15 July 2010.

2. "Professionals Weigh Graduate Skills, Weaknesses." *Design Intelligence*. Greenway Communications, 15 Nov. 2003. Web. 15 July 2010.

3. Ibid.

4. Ibid.

5. Priscilla March. "Networking for Students: a step-by-step guide." *boston.com*. The Boston Globe, 7 Mar. 2007. Web. 15 July 2010.

CHAPTER 4. WHAT IS AN ORGANIC FARMER?

1. JoNel Aleccia. "Pesticides in kids linked to ADHD." *msnbc.com*. MSNBC, 18 May 2010. Web. 15 July 2010.

2. Sue Shellenbarger. "Plumbing for Joy? Be Your Own Boss." *The Wall Street Journal Online*. The Wall Street Journal, 15 Sept. 2009. Web. 15 July 2010.

3. U.S. Bureau of Labor Statistics. "Farmers, Ranchers, and Agricultural Managers." *Occupational Outlook Handbook, 2010-11 Edition*. U.S. Bureau of Labor Statistics, 17 Dec. 2009. Web. 15 July 2010.

4. "Average Organic Farmer Salaries." *Simply Hired*. Simply Hired, Inc., n.d. Web. 24 Aug. 2010.

5. U.S. Bureau of Labor Statistics. "Farmers, Ranchers, and Agricultural Managers." *Occupational Outlook Handbook, 2010-11 Edition*. U.S. Bureau of Labor Statistics, 17 Dec. 2009. Web. 15 July 2010.

6. Allan Nation. "Salatin-designed Pastured Egg Production System Lowers Labor Cost." *The Grazier's Edge*. The Stockman Grass Farmer, n.d. Web. 20 Sept. 2010.

7. David Mitchell. Message to the author. 10 July 2010. E-mail.

8. Ibid.

9. Ibid.

SOURCE NOTES CONTINUED

CHAPTER 5. WOULD YOU MAKE A GOOD ORGANIC FARMER?

1. Becky Elder. Message to the author. 22 Apr. 2010. E-mail.

2. U.S. Bureau of Labor Statistics. "Biological Scientists." *Occupational Outlook Handbook, 2010-11 Edition.* U.S. Bureau of Labor Statistics, 17 Dec. 2009. Web. 15 July 2010.

CHAPTER 6. WHAT IS A PROFESSIONAL CONSERVATIONIST?

1. U.S. Bureau of Labor Statistics. "Conservation Scientists and Forresters." *Occupational Outlook Handbook, 2010-11 Edition.* U.S. Bureau of Labor Statistics, 17 Dec. 2009. Web. 15 July 2010.

2. Debra E. Blum. "Environmental Groups Chalk Up 2.7% Increase in Gifts, Report Finds." *The Chronicle of Philanthropy.* The Chronicle of Philanthropy, 8 June 2010. Web. 15 July 2010.

3. Ibid.

4. Irene Jones. Message to the author. 13 July 2010. E-mail.

5. Ibid.

6. Ibid.

7. "Environmental Advocacy: Academic Requirements, Professional Outlook." *EnvironmentalPrograms.net.* Environmental Programs.net, 1 Aug. 2003. Web. 15 July 2010.

CHAPTER 7. WOULD YOU MAKE A GOOD PROFESSIONAL CONSERVATIONIST?

1. Larry Tracy. "Can fear of public speaking actually make you a better speaker?" *HaLife.* Joe Hickman, 2006. Web. 15 July 2010.

2. "Greenpeace Attempts to Make Captain Paul Watson 'Disappear.' *Sea Shepherd Conservation Society.* Sea Shepherd Conservation Society, n.d. Web. 20 Sept. 2010.

3. "Greenpeace Denounces Sea Shepherd Society." *The Rewilding Institute.* n.p. Web. 15 July 2010.

CHAPTER 8. WHAT IS AN ALTERNATIVE ENERGY EXPERT?

1. "Peak Oil Primer." *Post Carbon Institute Energy Bulletin*. Post Carbon Institute, 23 Feb. 2010. Web. 15 July 2010.

2. "U.S. Department of Energy Analysis Finds That Wind Can Be Major Contributor to Energy Mix." *AWEA Newsroom*. American Wind Energy Association, 12 May 2008. Web. 15 July 2010.

3. "Wind Energy." *cn-friendtech.com*. Green Technology, n.d. Web. 21 Sept. 2010.

4. "Wind Energy Research & Demonstration." *Renewable Energy Initiatives: The Power of Wind*. University of Minnesota, 5 May 2008. Web. 21 Sept. 2010.

5. "ASES Green Collar Jobs Report Forecasts 37 Million Jobs from Renewable Energy and Energy Efficiency in U.S. by 2030." *American Solar Energy Society*. American Solar Energy Society, 15 Jan. 2009. Web. 15 July 2010.

6. Jerrolynn Kawamoto. Message to the author. 13 July 2010. E-mail.

7. Ibid.

8. Ibid.

9. Ibid.

10. Elizabeth Gehrman. "Hot Jobs in a Green Economy." *boston.com*. The Boston Globe, 18 Nov. 2007. Web. 20 Sept. 2010.

11. "Wind Power Industry." *Careers in Energy*. n.p. Web. 20 Sept. 2010.

CHAPTER 9. WOULD YOU MAKE A GOOD ALTERNATIVE ENERGY EXPERT?

1. Philip Su. "Effective Communication for Engineers." *The World as Best as I Remember It*. The World as Best as I Remember It, 24 July 2008. Web. 16 July 2010.

2. Ibid.

3. "Benefits of Geothermal Heat Pump Systems." *Energy Savers*. U.S. Department of Energy, 30 Dec. 2008. Web. 24 Aug. 2010.

INDEX

ABOUT THE AUTHOR

Courtney Farrell was once a career counselor and science instructor at Front Range Community College in Colorado. Now she is a full-time writer and the author of ten books for young people. She lives with her husband and sons on a ranch in the Colorado mountains.

PHOTO CREDITS